D0198207

A STUDY GUIDE FOR

The Freedom of Forgiveness

By
DAVID AUGSBURGER

By
KATIE FUNK WIEBE

MOODY PRESS
CHICAGO

CONTENTS

LESSON		PAGE
	Introduction	3
1.	I Can Never Forgive	7
2.	Then What Is Forgiveness?	9
3.	How Can I Forgive?	11
4.	Does Forgiving Take Time?	13
5.	Love, the Dragon-killer	15
6.	How to Live with a Tiger	17
7.	Why Should I Confess?	19
8.	Can Forgiveness Set Me Free?	21
9.	Tune-up for a Tired Marriage	23
10.	What's That in Your Eye?	25
11.	You Couldn't Care Less	27
12.	How Do You Want to Be Treated?	29
13.	Have You Only One Cheek?	31

© 1974 by
THE MOODY BIBLE INSTITUTE
OF CHICAGO

ISBN: 0-8024-2876-2

Printed in the United States of America

INTRODUCTION

Home Bible study groups. Church Bible study groups. Cell groups. Prayer groups. Church in the home. Sunday school class.

The name doesn't matter. What is important is that you and some other Christians have felt the need to come together for such an experience. You want to learn more about the Scriptures and how to make the truths of the Word work in daily life. You see a small group as an opportunity for the church to come alive.

No two small groups meet the same pattern, but if they are to survive successfully, they usually possess the characteristics given in the following paragraphs.

THE GROUP

Keep your group small enough for personal interaction, yet large enough for meaningful discussion. About twelve to fifteen members is probably a good size. It must meet regularly, preferably once a week. It must plan its meetings so that they start and stop fairly well on schedule and no member's babysitter has to wait past his bedtime.

LEADERSHIP

Call him a facilitator if you wish, rather than a leader. But someone is needed to give direction to the study. Where will your group meet? When? Whose turn is it to lead the discussion next time? What chapter will you consider next—the one you did not finish or the next one? A facilitator keeps these matters under control without being pushy.

A SENSE OF PURPOSE

Why study forgiveness? Why invest valuable time learning about the costly process of forgiveness? Any group which joins for a study of *The Freedom of Forgiveness* should have as its purpose the felt need of its members for a better understanding of one of the fundamental principles of life. Forgiveness is the bread of daily life.

COMMITMENT

The group must be committed to regular attendance and be willing to give up activities and entertainments, if need be, for the sake of the growth of the group. Commit yourselves to the study of this topic even when it becomes uncomfortable. Be open to the working of the Holy Spirit. In a small group the Spirit can work if each member is honest about himself, is concerned about others and their needs, and is willing to respect confidences. Deny yourselves the urge to pry into the inner lives of the other members to satisfy curiosity.

STRUCTURE SUFFICIENT TO ACCOMPLISH THE PURPOSE OF THE GROUP

Central theme. A main point of the chapter to be studied is summarized in the quotation from the book. (The page number given refers to *The Freedom of Forgiveness*.) The study is based upon this main thought. The group should not be allowed to wander from it to unimportant side issues.

Each member should read the complete chapter before the meeting, for greater participation.

Bible study. Read the suggested scripture passages together or individually. Ask yourselves what they say to you. What did they say to the persons for whom they were originally intended? Use more than one translation as you work with the Scripture. Include other materials on forgiveness, if you desire.

Discussion. What most people don't like about a discussion is monopolization of the time by one person, a wallowing in opinion in which there is no fresh input, or simply dead silence.

Forgiveness is a topic which can be discussed with worthwhile results only if it is made practical. Begin a discussion with some such question as "When I am hurt, I tend to avoid forgiving by—" or "When I am injured by another, my first impulse is—"

Ask everyone to contribute an answer. Then lead out from there. Encourage everyone to participate even if only by looking up and silently nodding his head. The final solution or answer to some person's problem may not come until a later session, but the effort to help that individual should continue from session to session. Avoid dropping a matter with "Well, we can pray about it."

Role playing. Role playing is recommended for any topic, but it is especially helpful when honest, objective opinions are desired on controversial subjects. Role playing may even encourage the most timid to say what he thinks without fear of criticism.

In role playing, each member participating assumes the identity of someone else (parent, teenager, wife, pastor, etc.). He does not need to agree with the viewpoint of the role he adopts. Acting out the problem situation should be informal and unrehearsed. The success of role playing depends to a large extent upon the way the actors identify themselves with the people they are portraying and lose their self-consciousness regardless of private opinions.

After the role playing, everyone (including players) discusses what has been presented. Sometimes it helps if during the discussion the players maintain their roles. If the suggested problems in this study guide do not relate sufficiently to the lives of your members, choose some other issue.

Project for the week. Encourage each member to pick a project for the week, related to forgiveness, which will keep the central theme in his thinking and further his understanding of it. This project can be the suggested one or one of his own choosing. Have each member report back to the group what transpired. Avoid making people feel the "false guilt" of which Augsburger writes, when they have nothing to say. Constantly encourage and support one another to carry over the purpose of the group into the experiences and relationships of the home, school, church, and community. Plan to learn more about forgiveness and what it means to be forgiven.

1

I CAN NEVER FORGIVE

SUMMARY

" 'He that cannot forgive others breaks the bridge over which he himself must pass if he would ever reach heaven; for everyone has need to be forgiven' " (p. 15) .

SCRIPTURE

Matthew 6:14-15; 18:21-35

QUESTIONS FOR DISCUSSION

1. Why should anyone forgive another person for a wrong which has been done him? Why not simply forget about it? Doesn't the process of forgiveness only add to the misery?
2. Wouldn't some type of punishment be more effective for an unfaithful wife or husband or a disobedient child instead of forgiveness?
3. What does it cost to harbor hatred? Can you think of a time in your own life when you bore someone a grudge for a long time and how it affected you physically, mentally, and socially?
4. How can parents make forgiveness an integral part of child training so that children learn how to forgive early in life?

5. How can forgiveness be made an integral part of the penal system in the work of rehabilitating legal offenders? How can Christians become a redemptive influence in society in this area of life?
6. How much of forgiveness depends on how much we love someone?

ROLE PLAYING

Mrs. Brown has impulsively bought a new dishwasher (or other item) when she and her husband had agreed they would postpone the purchase until the car payments were finished. The dishwasher has arrived. Role play the meeting of Mr. and Mrs. Brown.

PROJECT FORGIVENESS

For this week choose an easy project. Pick one person you find difficult to accept. All week listen to what that person has to say. What does he talk about? Make no judgment about him. Just listen! Why do you think he says the things he does? At the end of the week see if this exercise in listening has helped you learn something about forgiveness.

2

THEN WHAT IS FORGIVENESS?

SUMMARY

"Forgiveness is not mere politeness, tact or diplomacy!" (p. 19).

" 'No one ever really forgives another, except he bears the penalty of the other's sin against him' " (p. 21).

"Forgiveness is rare, hard, and costly: because it demands this kind of substitution" (p. 24).

SCRIPTURE

| 1 Peter 2:21 | Hebrews 2:9 | Colossians 3:13 |
| 2 Corinthians 5:19 | John 12:32 | Ephesians 4:32 |

QUESTIONS FOR DISCUSSION

1. When you forgive, aren't you overlooking evil, perhaps even encouraging it? How can forgiveness be made an active force in combating evil?
2. In what way does the principle of substitution operate in forgiveness? At the divine level? At the human level?
3. Should you ask forgiveness of a person who does not know he has offended you?

4. What should you do when others, by nurturing bitterness, make it hard for you to become a forgiving person?
5. Is it harder to forgive little offenses, like when a husband never cleans up after himself, or to forgive a major offense, like unfaithfulness?

ROLE PLAYING

Overeating by a daughter has created much tension in the home between mother and child. After a family picnic at which there was abundant food, the mother finds the daughter before the television set with a huge bowl of ice cream and some cookies. What does the mother say to her daughter? How can forgiveness and the principle of substitution be made a power to help both mother and daughter?

PROJECT FORGIVENESS

Get as close as possible to the person you have trouble accepting or loving. Ask to have coffee with that person several times. Sit beside him. If it is a member of the family, deliberately spend more time than usual with that person in conversation, work, or play. Report back what happened.

3

HOW CAN I FORGIVE?

Summary

"When we have learned to look about us with the loving eyes of Christ no man we see is unlovable, no man is beyond forgiving" (p. 30).

Scripture

Philippians 2:12-13   Colossians 3:12-14   1 John 4:20
1 Corinthians 13   Mark 8:36-37

Questions for Discussion

1. What is the difference between understanding and being understanding?
2. Does understanding necessarily mean agreeing with the other person? What is the difference between understanding and evaluating (with reference to clothes, hair styles, friends, personal habits)?
3. How can a person begin to see life from the other person's viewpoint—from the viewpoint of the one who feels injustice, hurt, and bitterness?
4. How can one learn to understand the needs of people who

11

are hard to live with: the ones who talk too much, who never talk, who exaggerate the truth, who dominate the discussion, who are quarrelsome, who are always late, who explode with anger at the least provocation, who are indecisive?

5. In what ways might full understanding of a person's situation breed contempt for that person?
6. How would you try to help someone who has become bitter and cannot forgive because justice has failed in some way—perhaps in a way related to his job, his family, his health, and so forth?

ROLE PLAYING

A fellow Christian comes to you to ask forgiveness because he stumbles over your freedom to attend occasional movies. How will you handle it?

PROJECT FORGIVENESS

Choose someone you have stereotyped as "unspiritual," "uncooperative," "disagreeable," "irritating," or "stubborn," and pray for that person every day this week. Try to find out something more about this person this week. Give the person some kind of a gift or token of yourself.

4

DOES FORGIVING TAKE TIME?

SUMMARY

"The man who follows Christ in life hurries to forgive. Quickly. Unhesitatingly. Immediately.

"Knowing the great value of time, he cannot afford to let it slip by in futile pain.

"He knows it is cheaper to pardon than to resent" (p. 33).

SCRIPTURE

Ephesians 4:31-32	1 Corinthians 13:5-8
Romans 15:7	Colossians 3:13

QUESTIONS FOR DISCUSSION

1. When should we forgive, when we are asked or before?
2. Why should forgetting follow forgiving?
3. Who should be the first to speak up after a misunderstanding, the one wronged or the wrongdoer?
4. Is it a sign of weakness to always be the first to be ready to forgive?
5. How can you help the awkwardness which develops after a reconciliation?

6. A person has made some slips of judgment, perhaps even deliberately deceived someone else. Later he regrets his action. How can he be helped to forgive himself? Is it harder to forgive others or to forgive self?
7. How can you forgive a person who does not actually deserve it and has no intention of changing his behavior?
8. What factors encourage bitterness to develop? How is bitterness related to self-pity? How can the following individuals overcome bitterness in their situations: a housewife with four small children and a salesman husband, a young man who has few dates, a businessman who is bypassed repeatedly for a promotion?
9. How would you help a parent to find forgiveness who feels a great burden of guilt because of a child who has rejected Christian standards of behavior?

ROLE PLAYING

Your seventeen-year-old son has been picked up by the police in a drug raid. You never knew of his involvement although you knew that the relationship between you and him was deteriorating. The police have phoned for you to come to the station to pick him up. How do you greet him? Where does forgiveness enter into a situation involving a legal offense?

PROJECT FORGIVENESS

Make a list of three things which make you angry or bitter. Ask yourself why you become angry. Are you afraid your reputation will suffer or that you will be inconvenienced or have to work harder? What would it cost to let go of these enjoyable angers? What might you gain in terms of better relationships? Report back to the group on at least one matter.

5

LOVE, THE DRAGON-KILLER

SUMMARY

"Anger is a valid, natural emotion. As an emotion, it is in itself neither right nor wrong" (p. 44).

"Anger as an explosion is always an unnecessary evil, hurtful to you and to others. Such anger is a violent desire to punish others, to inflict suffering or exact revenge" (p. 43).

SCRIPTURE

Mark 3:4-6   Ephesians 4:26-27, 31-32   James 4:1-2

QUESTIONS FOR DISCUSSION

1. Have everyone in the group list three or four situations with regard to self or other people, which are potential anger-producing situations in his home, place of employment, or neighborhood. How many of them are worth getting angry about? How many could be changed with a little effort? How many of them cause anger because of a personal reaction rather than because of a basically disagreeable situation?

15

2. How much is a person entitled to moods or general irritability because of physical problems, lack of sleep, overloaded schedule, or inherited tendencies?
3. What are some occasions when Christ exercised the emotion of anger? Can anger ever be righteous?
4. When was the last time you were angry about some right things for the right reasons and in the right way? Can you list at least one occasion?
5. If someone vents his anger against someone else while you are nearby, what should you do?
6. How should you handle anger in the home situation when it concerns children?

Role playing

How would you handle the following situations:

1. Your six-year-old has broken a favorite dish after having been told repeatedly that he should not touch it.
2. Your son comes in rather late after having promised to be in by your prearranged curfew. He is the bearer of the news that he has crumpled the front fender of the car and that it was his fault.
3. Your daughter admits to you that she is living with her boyfriend at college.

Project forgiveness

Spend at least one evening this week reading and studying about some subject that makes you angry or irritates you: hair styles, clothing styles, music, communes, et cetera. Try to read with an open mind. Use your local library. Report back at least one new fact you have learned which helped you understand this subject better.

6

HOW TO LIVE WITH A TIGER

SUMMARY

"To live with your hostility and anger-emotions, admit they are a problem to you. Don't just repress them, and don't just express them on others.

"Confess them. By owning up to God and to another honest person who is following Christ in life.

"Then open up—to God, to God's love, to God's truth, to God's Word. Let Him enter, control and cleanse your life to its depths with His healing love" (p. 62).

SCRIPTURE

Genesis 4:6-7	Proverbs 14:17, 29; 16:32; 19:11
Proverbs 15:1	James 5:16
James 1:19-20	Philippians 4:8

QUESTIONS FOR DISCUSSION

1. If temper is so closely related to temperament, should not people with hot tempers be held less responsible for their actions?

2. What can a person do to help himself understand his own actions and behavior?
3. How does one go about living with hostilities that are deeply implanted in one's character and are directed to no one in particular, such as political corruption, difficult past experiences, social problems, incongruities in church life?
4. At what point should a person get professional help for himself? For another?
5. Must anger always be released?
6. What are some ways you use to slow down your temper?

ROLE PLAYING

A friend has some basic hostilities toward the leadership in the church and toward some of the procedures related to finances. He wants to discuss these with you and in doing so reveals his anger about a number of matters. How will you handle it?

PROJECT FORGIVENESS

Do some intensive study this week about some aspect of our society (community, church, society as a whole) which should make you righteously angry. Read a book about it. Visit with someone involved in the problem. Do one positive thing in response: write a letter to the newspaper, speak to someone who has responsibility in this area, attend a meeting, et cetera.

7

WHY SHOULD I CONFESS?

SUMMARY

"We discover and experience release from our guilt in direct proportion to our willingness to face our sin, confess our sinfulness and accept forgiveness" (p. 68).

SCRIPTURE

Psalms 32:3-5; 51:3-4	1 John 1:9	Galatians 2:20
James 5:16	Romans 10:9-10	

QUESTIONS FOR DISCUSSION

1. When should a person confess a sin only to God? When to God and the person involved? When to God, the person involved, and the church or larger community?
2. Is there ever forgiveness without confession?
3. If a person repents honestly and turns away completely from his sin, must he confess at all?
4. What is the difference between confession and admitting that one has done the deed?
5. Confessing is humiliating. How does it help healing?

Role playing

Yesterday while you were quilting with members of the mission circle, you told them an unpleasant story about a neighbor. Today the story comes back to you much exaggerated. You also learn from another source that the story is only gossip and not true. Your neighbor comes over for a cup of coffee, unaware of what you have done. What will you do?

Project forgiveness

Discuss as a family or with your roommate a plan of action by which each one will accept personal responsibility for his actions and be willing to admit guilt and ask forgiveness. Memorize at least one verse about forgiveness.

8

CAN FORGIVENESS SET ME FREE?

SUMMARY

"The way to release begins with a change of attitude toward yourself and your sins and climaxes in a change of attitudes and actions toward God" (p. 74).

SCRIPTURE

Colossians 1:13-14	Matthew 21:31-32
Romans 3:19, 23	Proverbs 28:13
2 Corinthians 7:9-10	1 Peter 5:7
Acts 26:20	Psalms 40:10; 51:10, 13
Luke 13:5	Luke 4:18-19

QUESTIONS FOR DISCUSSION

1. What is the difference between true guilt and guilt as a conditioned response to childhood training by parents, teachers, and church leaders?
2. Why do some people have no guilt feelings about some significant type of misbehavior, while others suffer intensely for very minor misdemeanors?

3. How can we get rid of false guilt which is suggested to us by friends, foes, and family?

4. How can parents help their children to develop better self-images? How can an adult with a poor self-image be helped?

5. What is the difference between remorse, regret, and repentance?

6. How can a person get out of a vicious circle of guilt and regret that seems never to stop?

7. How much sharing should a person do regarding forgivegiveness of sin with other people? How can he avoid making the experience more important than continued growth?

8. Write down one statement that is an opinion you hold about something. Add a statement that expresses a prejudice of yours. Add a third that is a conviction or a belief related to the same general area of thought. Do they all agree?

9. How does labeling shut doors to understanding, friendship, and love? What would your attitude be if someone is introduced to you as a Roman Catholic? A Women's Libber? A Republican if you are a Democrat?

10. How involved should the church become in breaking down social prejudice in the community? What if a group in the church wants to become actively involved in promoting better relationships between the whites and the blacks (or in some other potential problem area in your community)? How would you advise them?

Project forgiveness

Plan to say something positive and complimentary to at least one person every day this week. Don't go to bed until you do.

9

TUNE-UP FOR A TIRED MARRIAGE

SUMMARY

"The husband and wife who discover the deepest levels of intimacy are those who give each other the completely unconditional acceptance of depth forgiveness. They gladly pay the cost of total forgiveness knowing that it brings a unity which is truly complementary and complete" (p. 90).

SCRIPTURE

Ephesians 4:26; 5:28-29, 25, 33

QUESTIONS FOR DISCUSSION

1. Is a marriage ever beyond repair? If communications become very difficult between a couple, should they separate?
2. Discuss the statement, " 'A good difficulty in your marriage can be marvelous. When you accept it as a challenge and resolve it, other things that are pulling you apart fade into the background' " (p. 90).
3. What can one partner do if the other person refuses to be involved in dialogue in an attempt to resolve tensions and conflicts?

4. How can communications be opened up again after a three-day silence has reigned supreme?
5. How can a couple resolve conflicts which arise out of problems related to child training?
6. What can a family do to encourage continuing openness among all members? Can the family devotional period be used effectively here?
7. If you see the marriage of some friends deteriorating, what should you do? At what point do you interfere and offer help?
8. To whom should a couple with marriage problems go for help?

ROLE PLAYING

Mr. and Mrs. Brown have a basic conflict. On weekends he likes to go hunting and fishing with his friends, while he expects her to stay home with the children. She would like to spend the time together as a family, especially because she has been home with the children all week and would like his support during the weekends. He has just made arrangements for a weekend hunting trip and tells her about it. Role play the resulting conversation.

PROJECT FORGIVENESS

Keep up-to-date accounts on anger and hostility in your home and at work all week. Did it help?

10

WHAT'S THAT IN YOUR EYE?

SUMMARY

"Only when a man attempts to judge in honesty, in humility and in charity is his own eye clear. Only then is the plank of an unloving, malicious or vengeful spirit removed. Only then is the beam of his own sinful actions and attitudes withdrawn. Then he can see his way clear to remove the splinter in the other's eye. Not to label it and give his brother a sore eye. But to offer the hand of help. And healing" (p. 100).

SCRIPTURE

Luke 4:18   1 Peter 4:8   Matthew 7:1-5

QUESTIONS FOR DISCUSSION

1. Discuss the statement, " 'Churchgoers are more prejudiced than the average; they are also less prejudiced than the average' " (p. 93).
2. Why does one person criticize another? Should one never offer criticism?
3. Why is it harder to accept criticism from a Christian than from a non-Christian?

4. Why is it harder to accept criticism from someone involved in the same area that you are in (music, teaching, etc.) than from someone outside the field?
5. What can the members of your group do to discourage criticism of your pastor? Of other church leaders?
6. How can your group work positively toward breaking down prejudice against blacks, Chicanos, welfare recipients, women, other denominations, young people with different lifestyles?
7. How many friends do you have outside your own "kind"? Is this the way you would like it?

ROLE PLAYING

The organist in church enjoys playing classical church music. One small group in church supports her choice of music. Another group prefers gospel songs for preludes and postludes. Some individuals are very vocal about a small folk group in church, which uses guitars with bass and drums. The tension is mounting. Role play a church music committee meeting.

PROJECT FORGIVENESS

Report back to the group examples of labeling (prejudging on the basis of one characteristic) you have overhead this week. How many of these labels were valid? How often was a person labeled stuck-up because he was rich, lazy because he was poor, inferior because he was of another race, et cetera?

11

YOU COULDN'T CARE LESS

SUMMARY

"Neglect is the greatest sin of all. To neglect God's offer of new life, to neglect God's free gift of salvation, to neglect God's power for living, to neglect doing God's work in our world, to neglect being God's people today—is the sin that damns a man forever. And by his own choice" (p. 108).

SCRIPTURE

| Revelation 3:15-16 | 1 John 3:17-18 | Hebrews 2:3 |
| James 4:17 | Matthew 25:45 | |

QUESTIONS FOR DISCUSSION

1. How can a person combat neutrality and apathy in his own life with regard to social problems? Can you draw up a plan of action?
2. A neighbor's son is involved in drugs. You know it. Your neighbor doesn't. You also know that he doesn't like nosy neighbors. What should you do? When does telling him about his son become interference? When is it love?
3. How much more than humanists should Christians accept

moral responsibility to save life, to serve others, to share help? Why does it seem that the church sometimes falls into second place in this regard?

4. What is the proper balance between evangelism and reaching out in deliberate acts of love?

5. In what area of society has the church sinned by silence?

ROLE PLAYING

Your daughter tells you that she is pregnant and that she doesn't know who the father is. Role play the conversation between her and you, her parents. What would it mean to take the way of self-giving love in this situation?

PROJECT FORGIVENESS

Make a concerted effort this week to pull yourself off the comfortable couch of apathy and indifference to problems around you by some specific action related to some definite need. Offer to run for office for some organization; give a donation to some cause you would ordinarily not contribute to; write a letter of protest; attend a meeting; find some new way you can use your gifts; open your home to a Bible study; visit the people in your retirement home.

12

HOW DO YOU WANT TO BE TREATED?

SUMMARY

" 'Second-mile religion' is a matter of love. You've traveled the first mile when you've learned to love your friendly neighbor. You face the second mile when you decide to love your enemy, adversary or competitor" (p. 115).

SCRIPTURE

Matthew 7:12; 22:37, 39; 6:14-15; 5:39-41

QUESTIONS FOR DISCUSSION

1. What should you do with a person who takes up your limited time with long phone calls or long visits, mostly because it seems he does not have enough to do?
2. Is it possible to use the golden rule in a business situation without being forced into bankruptcy?
3. A poor family in your community has been the recipient of countless gifts of food, clothing, and funds, yet there seems to be no evidence of progress in the home. The chil-

dren are still as poorly clothed and show evidence of malnutrition. People are refusing to give because it is like pouring water through a sieve. Is it the Christian's concern how his gifts are used?

4. If a person cannot do something willingly when he is requested to do it, should he do it at all (teach a Sunday school class, join a plowing bee for a sick member, etc.)?

5. How can a person today make more time for "second-mile living"? Is it even reasonable to suggest it might work in our busy type of living?

ROLE PLAYING

1. A young man who cannot hold down a job for more than several months asks you to sign a note for him for a new car.

2. The neighbor comes to borrow your lawn sweeper when he has not yet returned a garden hose and some clippers he borrowed last week.

3. The secretary at the desk next to yours insists on chainsmoking. Smoking gives you a headache.

4. Your husband has the habit of flopping onto the couch each evening after supper, and you would like his help in doing the dishes and putting the children to bed.

5. You find out that your wife has been secretly drinking at home by herself while you are at work. She has become an alcoholic. You are a deacon in the church.

How would you wish to be treated in each case?

PROJECT FORGIVENESS

Watch for the first opportunity to travel the second mile this week. When someone asks you to do something for him, do something additional. Report back to the group what this was and what happened. Your child may ask you to play a game of ball when you wanted to read the paper.

13

HAVE YOU ONLY ONE CHEEK?

SUMMARY

"An age of violence needs men at peace with God and man. Men who know Christ truly by following Him daily in life.

"Men who give the defenseless love of Christ, but are always on the offensive. Always serving. Always concerned about the other. Always giving themselves for the good of others. Always turning the other cheek for the sake of others.

"That is the way of Christ. The way of forgiving love" (p. 126).

SCRIPTURE

Exodus 21:23-25	Matthew 5:38-39; 44-45
Leviticus 24:19-20	1 Peter 2:23
Deuteronomy 19:21	2 Peter 3:11, 14

QUESTIONS FOR DISCUSSION

1. Discuss the statement: " 'Americans not only condone violence, we love it. We love to fight' " (p. 118) . Why is violence popular among Americans? Consider such things as television, movies, novels, athletics, car racing.

2. Jesus spoke about turning the other cheek. Does this mean a person should turn the other cheek also when the blow is not physical but psychological?
3. When does a person have the right to stand up for his rights or his reputation?
4. When should a person defend the rights of another person?
5. Nonviolence is sometimes confused with spinelessness. When might this be true? When is nonviolence a positive constructive force?
6. With regard to matters decided by political process, has the nonviolent person no recourse to protest at any time?
7. What is the difference between defenseless love and defensive living?

ROLE PLAYING

One of the secretaries you work with has just made a cutting remark about another secretary in her presence. You take it from here, for you are close enough to hear what is going on.

PROJECT FORGIVENESS

Make this Stop Gossip week. Every time you hear someone speaking derogatorily about someone else, either deliberately change the conversation to another subject or provide the true facts.